Parts of love

New Women's Voices Series, No. 139

poems by

Dina Paulson-McEwen

Finishing Line Press
Georgetown, Kentucky

Parts of love

New Women's Voices Series, No. 139

Copyright © 2018 by Dina Paulson-McEwen
ISBN 978-1-63534-452-3 First Edition
All rights reserved under International and Pan-American Copyright Conventions. No part of this book may be reproduced in any manner whatsoever without written permission from the publisher, except in the case of brief quotations embodied in critical articles and reviews.

Publisher: Leah Maines
Editor: Christen Kincaid
Cover Art and Design: Pria Borg-Marks, @priabee
Author Photo: Bree Gant, gant.studio

Printed in the USA on acid-free paper.
Order online: www.finishinglinepress.com
also available on amazon.com

Author inquiries and mail orders:
Finishing Line Press
P. O. Box 1626
Georgetown, Kentucky 40324
U. S. A.

Table of Contents

Canadian geese 1

Neue 2

Sonohysterogram with propofol 3

New brain and old brain 5

Morning party 7

Flesh 8

The ritual 9

They have been called in to clean up the blood 12

Parts of love 13

I am sorry to alienate the person I love you 14

Untitled 17

So-so 18

Salon 21

Thoroughfare 22

Unhinged 24

Soft 25

Barefoot 26

Pop meet Joni Mitchell 27

Founding 29

*For my grandmother,
who lines my heart*

*In memory of Maya,
September 8, 1970—May 11, 2017*

Canadian geese

Our white blood cells come
and someone remembers
to scatter around air

A necessary, flimsy envy
fills our brains as we
hustle for maps and medals

A grass-based camaraderie,
and knowledge about boundaries
thousands of years old

But their dictionaries
have not faded and ours,
we forget nearly all

This noise
(us winning and them winning)
looks like

c   n
  o   e
        f
                       t   t
        i

And rust handprints
color us red
forget-me-nots

And you lift my
dress, whistle at
the wind, and take me

Neue

I will let you linger if
you lift up my fanon if
holding tight is privilege if
benzoline is metaphor if
to pierce means to cut if
unravelling happens if
we eat our recompense by hand if
we decide to agitprop if
we wet our fingers with mib if
we creep out the fancy city if
we leven any malachite we see if
we take up an instrument
say, the kamaicha

Sonohysterogram with propofol

We move to michigan because of freckle-light
latitude specs. baby-making. the reportage is positive:
no chance of our dream fenestrating.

Start by:
blushing. We are part luxurious. Twenty ferrets grab pulleys to open up my legs. I breathe about once per night. one part clara burton one part one thousand yellows.

Stained windows, or toes between my hip bones like you—the shaved skull of homeskin: gold finger and clipboard who is not our fucking therapist. *Mail attention to: ART Lab.* Do you see why I mate with dogs? <u>We moved here for hospitals</u>. to ensure our girlbodies would fuck and bend and inseminate as they were meant to.

The therapist notices: you are disturbed by intrusion. become, reticently, a womanblob. womanparts pussed through strategic stenographic
scarring

But mostly, I am ecstatic.
Propofol—the drug Jessica Jones used to put Killgrave in solitary confinement.
How she stabbed that shit into his neck, and everyone fell over lo mein.

Fearless Ms. Jones, I understand now: this is total intoxication of nothingness.

A catheter and saline balloon are put inside, but at this point, I do not remember anything. Later, after cringeworthy wake-up cooing to my boo, I hear *everything looks good tubes untied uterus clear*

Bloating, cramping, spotting, sensitized nipples, dissipate over a few weeks. Preparationnecessaryforperformance. Thank you so much for intravening, music, and invitees. *But why,* said the nurse, *are you shaking when you will be sleeping soon?*

Afterwards, expect to:

I: *bye*, you
albatross

II: stumble, when bumbleberries fly

II: be easy:
footprints. walk around like cotton candy
lubed and whiplash

III: pretend: *I never
went anywhere...*   IV: become a steak carver: *where I could not
perseverate on you at all*

New brain and old brain

                    that the body will heal
              its particular way of healing

                                  as a sunset
                                  /wavy from eggs

    your heart tucked
    in by ribbons of brain

                where cells smoke *sencha*

                      *

hearts that landscape rhubarb raw and rhubarb baked. attempts are washed by southern heat.

                    *

at *night*, repose and eviscerate. erotic romance (we take in forms.)

    how?
    a coward at the end is a coward at the beginning, only the premise of
        movement.

                    *

we are bandits **we** arrive through **we** thick nostril **we** on sleds **we** resist resistance **we** have heirs
with teflon hooves.

                    *

disoriented status: we begin to heal but there is longing. with tweezers, we place each other's jaws, and some like musk; for example, feet.

do not forget we came to heal.
we as fruit pickers **we** as regulators **we** as brackish **we** drank naranja.

Morning party

Hips shake out, tight. We laugh,
look, you cusp
me and pantomime :

  Love cheeks, drawing two circles in the air.

I hold up my socks :

Silliness : bed lines in the living room :
your arms
a caftan
for me to crawl into.

I get up earlier than you, in water and jewelry.

This face I know, pillow held and
breathes softly | one eye open | dragon-like.

You dressed up nicely.
(pause)
Your hair is long.
(pause)
Bounty
(pause)

!Morning party!

Your face scrunches and :

I will be your favorite.

Flesh

We layer ourselves
in robes and ropes
with all this flesh
we have dug up

The ritual

The ritual was clear: we would go to the river, we would sunbathe, we would sandbathe. This was when we were in Pangea. The ritual said: we go to the river, we dip our bodies into the tunnels that keep us from the spaces where the sunlight hits the ground and how it appears in the sky, otherwise burning us. In incandescence and probability. And then we spread out our towels and check each other for ticks. We check between our feet, we make sure that centipedes do not cross our toes, we make sure our eyes lock with one another's. We used to be joined but now we are not, but we pretend we still are. Then, we sandbathe.

We dip each other's heads into the sand and move the head around as if we were in water, swishing it back and forth among the crushed up particles, sand petals, with our hands, as if washing a container or someone's hair appliance, but in this case, it is the thing inside, *the head,* what is covered with hair and scrawls and electoral delicacies that we are washing slowly from side to side. Gun metal, a new color for festivities, is also a good description for how we banter.

As a butter churner does.

We take each head into our hands, settling our fingers into the crevices above the ears and gently guide the head to the right, to the left, then, carefully, lift up the head with our fingers and let it fall down! fast into the water, give it a spin right at the end so it falls into the water, hard, on its backside. We want to wash each other thoroughly and the water will seep inside we know, if we whip at certain intervals.

The heads, once rung out after teasing the river, its beds warmed by sun, are taken slowly through sand as if on a journey we had not decided we would take but were already on, then placed side by side by a large, Goofy hand. There is a holiday coming and on this holiday we will determine a lot.

There is sound above our heads, coming for our heads. We feel assured that ritual has been enough, assured we got out extra pieces with q-tips we imagined we had in our hands when we flipped—there might have been some invisible bird or insect or slippery thing that attached itself to our hands in that moment (hidden) and made that flip, an insert, to help us along. Or we could have done all this while splitting pumpkin seeds, roasting them, setting them out for display, becoming sellers of gourds and marketers and harvesters and fresh entrepreneurs. The amount of force it takes to flip a heavy head—but this is the story of ritual, not of solace, not of grievance. This is about how heads become what are they are becoming.

Once rung out, now hanging out, we are set towards each other, reminding we used to be. Some feel strongly, fill their glasses; others glee, others fear for what they see (repeating) unsure patterns, if old patterns look breakable, can be infiltrated. Are breathable. It is possible two heads can lay in the same space and lick each other where the water temperature is low (we are in the orderly room) and the podiums wet with sweat from those who stare curiously, introduce themselves hurriedly, elatedly. There are seldom parties nobody wants to be invited to.

We start to forget we, or they, might have been joined at one point. We cannot help but focus on who is balding. The shapes of all heads are incongruous with each other yet smell the same: timber. A new-age jewelry piece waiting for an owner, a slice of heat in the form of cornbread you smash in your hand that will be delivered, like a holiday, fast to the person, in its crumbles, who says its name correctly. Sweet bread. Bodies as bread. *The first land. Doughy.* Not as exciting as assumed. The audience likes to be quiet. The audience likes to be uproarious, the audience likes puppies, and sweaters, and questions, and falling. The audience is interested in remembering what is in their interest.

The heads are banging each other, velvet everywhere. Their hairs make bold their stories and ancestors, more porous, allowed in the present day to fill up on others. Our heads are spinning.

How do we keep track of these heads, and our heads, and the heads who have sweated?

And this goes around and dizzies, someone tastes like candy, candy falls for everyone, and there is a single thumb that decides. Candy gets others high and buries into teeth without discrimination. Candy eyes see ships. See blocks. See the stabs over doors.

There are eyes that come looking, wild, at the heads. They want to decide if the heads' porosity is something to infiltrate (or not). But while listening, from their heads, full from history about love and where was / is *not love,* where has been joy and what can we make it, clears. And then we see joy, as a determinant, pushing back continents, a smile that gives, falls, finds, decides it needs a catcher and so an attender, and an attendant, and an audience. And these heads are lolling and the amount of time it takes to continue the amount of living and the amount of head we can see, in a way, gets smaller. And how we write about this is the next part and will end up in our pockets as grains of sandbaths and lines of sun droppings and names that translate as faith and any natural bodies made of water nearby. And these will line up when you say *ritual* and our blood is electoral and our hearts are fired black.

They have been called in to clean up the blood

I see the blood on the floor. Is that your blood? I do not know. It is dry like it has been here for awhile. I do not remember when your last surgery was—it has been a blur from the sidelines, you heading straight for the goal: life. Did you bleed at first? Or at the end? When they inserted the tubes in the middle and a part of you spilled out a little bit? A lot out? Was there no one to catch you? It is not your blood; it is the blood of the floor. It lives here. This is the blood that remains. This is the blood that came from someone at some time and stayed; it is no matter when it arrived or from whom. The spots are spread out. Drop drop splaaaat. Little. Circles. Ovaldrops. Splaaaat. Someone had a lot of emotion; maybe it was the doctors. I would like to think if the blood had a chance it might have a sensitivity closer to mine, one that would know a specked, scuffed linoleum floor would be too disdainful to hold me. No, I would say, as I made my way to the floor, mad rushing, I will not SPLAAAAT here. I will not land here. I will not stain here. I will not become a part of here. I would like to think this is not your blood, but I know better.

There is a party and the doctors are here—this is my version. They paint pictures of themselves, and one has red hair. She adds a dollop to her head and splaaaat, one clot of thick paint dives to the floor. She does not notice and, later, on their way out as they collect their tonic waters and popcorn, she steps in it, crocs slick with soda, thinning out the blood. The clot becomes opaque. It dries this way. In reality, the next day, someone in a uniform comes into the room. They have been called in to clean up the blood. I hear there is some blood to be cleaned here, they ask? Yes, the patient says. Can you please move out of the way? We move out of the way—me with my legs, you, gingerly, with the help of a technology machine. I am so sorry for you. But I knew it was your blood the whole time, there was never any question. But I write because I hoped the blood was not yours. I take my seat again and notice there is still one spot of blood there. A piece of you so stubborn it will stay on and so, your blood stays here. There is blood here. Your blood and a beating heart.

Parts of love

I

We went to the lake, formed by river run-off, where you decided to create
a new sneaker, the type to slip on and off.
Look, it is your heart, you said—
it can go in, go out, have lunch
all while
it is happening.

II

The first time I ate you, I felt full to my toes.   The first time I ate you, parts of me were more
love than they had ever been.   Parts of love, I said, about these ounces, pouches of you, that were in me.

I am sorry to alienate the person I love you

I asked Krishna and
that awesome Francis; God
whom Moses talked to,
the one my Torah
teacher wrote out
like this—
g (space) hyphen (space) d
because it was too holy

(I wrote God this way until
I was a teenager because
it looked like an art project,
something to jump through,
a song that continues to be played)

I called on these characters
and the Torah teacher
to ask about loving and longing—
why loving gets
stuck in the back of my throat
when all I want to do < my voice
begins its stucked-ness > is love

Loving and longing do not un-stick
easily, one reminded me—
you need to be stuck, said another—and
God grinned,
and my old teacher
reached down and touched my hand

Find that place of throat, she said,
and make the hardest love—the
biggest windstorm you have felt inside—
come out of you then swallow you
as Jonah was gulped with hunger,

providence,
intention, and a goal

my eyes widened—I exhaled hard,
and nodded, *and then,* I asked?

and then, she said, once you are
inside, feel the walls (they are
braille) poke out that tongue of yours
to find the other tongue
(and everything became solid
but wet, like a slide, when
these two touched)

and then, lick those walls around you,
and then lick the other's feet, *and then,* lick
your feet, *and remember,*
you will need to twist
your head because
some parts are harder to get to,
to clean off, than others

and this will probably take days,
because your tongue
is not used to poking on purpose,
to the stretch it takes to stroke
another's, *and remember,* your sweat
from your effort to get there
must be dry, and you must only bring
sweet, soft breath, *and so,* it will take days,
because you will need to do this
again and again and again

once I am done with bending,
licking, welding my tongue with
yours, hands curved as a
horse's back, I have stepped
on myself, right foot over left foot,
all this to keep up
the room of hashem

Then I will feel where you
live—bold, as an eagle,
the underbelly too loose, with
dots around your lips I see you,
like me—

I have only to offer my tongue;
raw hands to grasp onto yours,
my tongue, like a lizard, and
feet swelling as I step over
myself, hold onto myself,
to be there soon to you

Untitled

a heart a round a knapsack a jewel an endometric thing a ladder |
a heart a knapsack a jewel an endometric thing a ladder a round |
a heart a jewel an endometric thing a ladder a round a knapsack |
a heart an endometric thing a ladder a round a knapsack a jewel |
a heart a ladder a round a knapsack a jewel an endometric thing

So-so

So-so go black beads
over black beans
over subway lines
ti voglio
as quiet
as mama hippos
in Mpumalanga

So-so is water
suckling and our
bodies tricking out
on the body buffet:

chiffon

lace

lemon

hooked

tart

waits to irrigate—

        as a bird flicks scars off its shoulder and asks about the quality of
        water   specifically, what are we going to do about it

because stuff
got patented
così così
with semen
and lemon
ho detto mil veces

the shape
of our shul—
lenient—
and our knapsacks—
japanese (but
who could blame
us) and
our ballots come
down with
party syndrome

solamente
la fruta, per piacere

Pre-ceptance

    -our mixture of pretend and acceptance
    -as mocha drinking moths
    -in a monosyllabic
    -monastery

and our legs
cannot close
without chiffon
ti abbraccio
cannot pray
high enough
ti bacio di più
pan-geographic enough
panther-strident
with-pitchfork-dipped
in-velvet-enough
amore mio
but we breed
our friendships
like tart-feasting
rabbits

poi, mi chiami,

okay?

Notebooks made
from pressing flowers
into lace and pollen
into points passed
from elders
to the leaves of our pages

"Big" describes "essence"

ti mando tutto,

dopo

when we cluster
when we shuffle
our faces with
dill, turmeric,
and hooked
dreamcatchers

Salon

When we rise up, we will live in Vortex, horse around in verse. A silhouette who looks like us, trains like us, walks like us, offers aperitivi in alternating, monosyllabic languages. Everyone feels underwater or inside Gertrude Stein's salon. We rub toes, simultaneous brain and erotica. There are cliffs, bastions, cherries, bells.

Thoroughfare

I.

for candlelight, include:
toes and melon cuts. in-laws
referred to as "mastiff."

II.

on wednesday, upholster.
on thursday, suck leftover lollies
stuck on loveseats.

III.

for snails, include:
margarine. meta lies. fantasy
figures who cook me dinner,
make love to me, swoon me,
when you are unable to.

for excuses, include:
i am not allowed too many
orgasms. you are not allowed
to count.

IV.

for realism, include:
sanctimoniously rig
us up. the ganges river.
wax chairs.

V.

for love, include:
binoculars. oprah.
megabytes of
forgiveness,
a vase of memory
strapped to our heads,
like miners. one rsvp card.
it passes between our hands
until it becomes liquid.

Unhinged

where the one thing left over
was sun and the one place
unmade was above and the
one sect we called home was
our mouths | when the place
we skipped over said | go over
our mounds and our mouths
and our mothers and ourselves
and we said okay
because our heaven
is constant dancing

Soft

Aphrodisiacs allow
watching
and learning :

A soft
scream :

*The sum of empathy
from inside parts*

And say :

I love you : and : *Thank you for being here* :

And *Thank you*

:

And *I love you*

Barefoot

Among silky
blues the color
I love most :

you : a peppermint pie :

you : of pinging
bodies to bodies

you : of wrists and
ankles : you of
lanterns

us : in barefoot a and
b over boiling sweets

Pop meet Joni Mitchell

And just like that, their ties did not matter. The left hand gripping its left side so tight while the right-side hails frantic. A reaching millennial.

Can you catch me?

Their ties did not matter because everything had been broken a hundred times over, broken itself over itself like glass falling down the stairs. In the same action (Is Hurt) (And Hurting).

Broken not in the way that it will never be fixed but broken so that fixing will take so long that breathing to get there will break each of us again. (the double breaking, the Infinity break).

One sets up a scouting plant to look out for the other, a traditional way of saying, let me wear your boots for a thousand miles. Pop meet Joni Mitchell, you owe her… a place where you take turns looking and sometimes sandwich-in the other by planting yourself on their lap. Also you arrange a cushy chair for the two of you near the multicolored rafters and buoys that fit each day of the week and a screen that affixes itself to radio waves—this is a bad-pun stand-in for all the possibilities of emotion you might encounter. Then you set up friends at each station so the person you love always has possibility to be narrator and listener, to be smothered, kept up. And then you set up the weather so the air feels like velvet but tastes like lemon.

—This helps with the rush of brokenness that comes as fast as city summer. Because the first part of brokenness happens where broken parts are sown. Because of re-breaking and re-setting, there are castles and suitcases, dried lavender and shards, vegan monsters, and made machinery—pieces of all these (because they have been rubbed down by our legs **hard**) are strewn about the lawn area. When we first lived in the lawn area, our names were etched into each strand, narrow enough to hold all our syllables. just l-o-v-e

But then, brokenness is a process because imagine—this lawn was created in mania and intent and since has become so large. Its images, the leftovers and the new shapes, like upcyclers in Berlin.

Founding

As they do, adolescent—
unsubscribe by peeling
asphalt from creative
space—point to things
known about,
dreamt about, things souls
are set aside to rest about

Say Wicca books, our organs warm
up the shape of doilies.
Unhook
your peer, your own
garrulous master
ship, its mandate and
its followers

A letter stuffed down
pulled from
geese throat, whether
that signal you sent—
a dagger of fire
amongst all the black—
will bring me home

Additional Acknowledgments

Thank you firstly to Finishing Line Press—specifically to Leah Maines, Kevin Maines, Christen Kincaid, Mimi David, Jennifer Winebrenner, Jackie Steelman, and Joe. Your publishing expertise, professionalism, and cheer from the beginning through production (Leah mails cards of congratulations!) made for a beautiful process of book making. Thank you so much for supporting women writers and poets through your New Women's Voices Series and for keeping small presses significant messengers of literature.

Thank you to Abbie Copeland, Marthe Reed, Robin Richardson, and Eileen R. Tabios for reading this manuscript and offering your responses. I admire each of you, your poetics, and your leadership in the writing world, particularly for women writers, so much and am honored you shared yourselves with me and *Parts of love* . Thank you to my heart friend and writing mentor, Cheryl Forbes. Without you, my mind and fingers would be incomplete.

Thank you to Detroit for opening up your spaces and letting me walk and sit and read and write in you.

Dina Paulson-McEwen is the author of *Parts of love* (Finishing Line Press, 2018), a 2017 finalist in the Finishing Line Press New Women's Voices Chapbook Competition. Her work appears in *Flash Fiction Magazine, FlashFlood, Minola Review, Dying Dahlia Review, The Ham Free Press, The Hungry Chimera*, the anthology *Evidence of Fetus Diversity*, and elsewhere. Her poetry has been exhibited at Hudson Guild Gallery and San Juan Capistrano Library. She is assistant managing editor at *Compose | A Journal of Simply Good Writing*, editor at *Flash Fiction Magazine*, and editor extraordinaire with youth writers at Uptown Stories. In 2017, she launched Aqua Editing to collaborate with creative thinkers, including educators, entrepreneurs, and fiction writers, on storytelling their work. Prior to Aqua Editing, she worked in communications with education organizations in the U.S. and overseas and taught literacy in English and Spanish to youth and adult learners. She holds a B.A. in Writing & Rhetoric from William Smith College, an M.A. in International Educational Development from Teachers College, Columbia University, and a Certificate of Completion for the Summer Writing Program at the Jack Kerouac School for Disembodied Poetics—Naropa University. She lives in Princeton, New Jersey.

www.ingramcontent.com/pod-product-compliance
Lightning Source LLC
LaVergne TN
LVHW041507070426
835507LV00012B/1398